LINDY LEE:
SONGS ON MILL HILL

poems by

Kimberly J. Simms

Finishing Line Press
Georgetown, Kentucky

LINDY LEE:
SONGS ON MILL HILL

ACKNOWLEDGMENTS

Thanks to the editors of *Aji Magazine* (NM: Aji, 2017), *The South Carolina Review* (Clemson, SC: Clemson UP, 2015), The Blue Collar Review (Norfolk, VA: Partisan Press, 2006), *Kakalak* (Charlotte, NC: Main Street Rag, 2006), *The Millennial Sampler of South Carolina Poetry* (Greenville, SC: Ninety-Six Press, 2005). Also thank you to the Poetry Society of South Carolina and the York County Arts Council for recognizing these poems through their award programs.

Deepest gratitude to the Friends of the Carl Sandburg Society and the Metropolitan Arts Council for the gift of time to write this book.

Publisher: Leah Maines

Editor: Christen Kincaid

Cover Art: Kimberly J Simms, *Brick Walls* Block Print, Acrylic, Paper.

Photos by Lewis Hine: Library of Congress, Prints & Photographs Division, National Child Labor Committee Collection. (In order of appearance). LC-DIG-nclc-01581, LC-DIG-nclc-01451, LC-DIG-nclc-00217, LC-DIG-nclc01550, LC-DIG-nclc-01476, LC-DIG-nclc-02978, LC-DIG-nclc-01472, LC-DIG-nclc-01546, LC-DIG-nclc-00246, LC-DIG-nclc-01338, LC-DIG-nclc-01556, LC-DIG-nclc-02642, LC-DIG-nclc-01345, LC-DIG-nclc-02003, LC-DIG-nclc-01638, LC-DIG-nclc-01441, LC-DIG-nclc-01544, LC-DIG-nclc-01455, LC-DIG-nclc-02835, LC-DIG-nclc-01471, LC-DIG-nclc-01636.

Author Photo: Elbert Ivory Photography

Cover Design: Kimberly J Simms

Printed in the USA on acid-free paper.
Order online: www.finishinglinepress.com
also available on amazon.com

Author inquiries and mail orders:
Finishing Line Press
P. O. Box 1626
Georgetown, Kentucky 40324
U. S. A.

Table of Contents

"Bibb Mill No. 1 Many youngsters here. Some boys were so small they had to climb up on the spinning frame to mend the broken threads and put back the empty bobbins.
Location: Macon, Georgia."

Notes by Lewis Hine as preserved by the
National Child Labor Committee Collection.

"People said that [on payday]
frogs sat on the river
and hollered,
'Balance due, balance due.'"

Alice Evitt

Mill Worker
as quoted in
Like a Family (Chapel Hill: UNC 1987).

For Jeremy Gibbs, Andy Gibbs, Lee Wright, and the community members who shared their personal remembrances of the textile era. Thank you to my parents Pauline Magee and John Simms who have always encouraged and supported my poetry. Thank you to William Wright, Ryan Van Cleave, Wayne Chapman, Joel McCollough, and Vera Gomez for their support and their keen attention to these poems. Special thanks to Lynda Bouchard, my publicist, for her guidance.

❧

In special recognition of Lewis Hine (1874 – 1940) whose poignant photographs of child mill workers are included from his work for the National Child Labor Committee from the Southern Piedmont region from 1908 – 1915. These photos are now held by the Library of Congress. His work was instrumental in leading to child labor laws which were enacted as part of the Fair Labor Standards Act of 1938. Since Hine often gained access to mills on false pretenses, such as being a fire inspector or bible salesman, the young workers featured in these pictures are unidentified.

BALANCE DUE

"A little spinner in the Mollahan Mills, Newberry, S.C."

Shift Bell: A Found Poem

1890. Male. Loom Fixer. 13 cents per hour.
1890. Male. Weaver. 6 cents per hour.
1890. Female Weaver. 6 cents per hour.
1890. Female. Spinner. 3 cents per hour.

Wakeup Bell. 4:30 a.m.
Breakfast Bell. 5:15 a.m.
Call Bell. 5:45 a.m.
Work Bell. 6:00 a.m.
Curfew Bell 9:00 p.m.

1914. Male. Overseer. 35 cents per hour.
1914. Male. Weaver. 7 cents per hour.
1914. Female. Weaver. 6 cents per hour.
1914. Female. Spinner. 3 cents per hour.

Wakeup Bell. 4:30 a.m.
Breakfast Bell. 5:15 a.m.
Call Bell. 5:45 a.m.
Work Bell. 6:00 a.m.
Call Bell 5:45 p.m.
Shift Bell 6:00 p.m.

"I arouse the slothful,
I call the people to work.
I announce the Sabbath Day,
I warn ye how your time passes away.
Serve God, therefore, while life doth last,
And say, '*Gloria in Excelsis Deo.*'"

LINDY LEE'S SONG
1916

We grew up with feet in red dirt,
knew nothin' but the rushin'
of our little creek. We grew taters,
tobacco, okky and maters. All us

littl'ins helped Ma and Daddy pickin'.
Sometimes when I smell honey
as March starts to warm
I turn towards the purple trees

and think of that little farm.
When we moved on the mill hill,
I saw the electric lights.
I dreamed of yellow ribbons in my hair.

I figured we were rich.
Didn't matter no more about rain.
Six days a week I stand at the frames,
dreamin' the songs of pulsing cicadas.

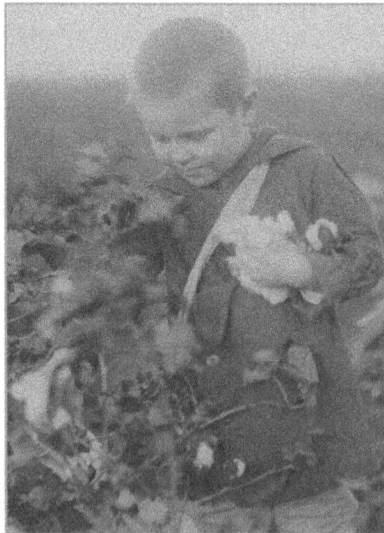

DADDY'S SILENCE
1918

Silence is a pause between shifts,
a Sunday dawn. It ain't a commodity
but it's rarer than gold.

Farmers got a sense about snakes
they hear the tremor of the grass,
the slight zither.

But here, the looms are so stretched out
they shriek and jerk like sinners
in a circle of fire.

I know the sound of moth's wings.
I've heard the first cricket of spring,
a lifetime back I held the clarity of silence.

DIP

Doctor said it would make me grow.
That first time chaw flipped my stomach.
But all the mill girls dip.
My sisters swear the thick stew
keeps out the lint.

When my aunts came up
they had spittoons.
Now we sisters bring
our own little jars.
I never seen a girl puff
a cigarette.
The townies tell—
it is unladylike.

WHITTLING

Sundays the men lean around the porch,
their little knives just going, whittling
pirate knives, rifles, raccoons, bears:
laughing about the slide in last week's

baseball game and the catch that sent
Bud over backwards. The minute a fish
is finished, a young'un is asking for the toy.
You get so used to doing, it's hard to stop.

Men find some silence in every chisel
of the blade. Each whittled bit
individual design, expression
free from a textile machine.

SPEED UPS

It started slow like a skittering millipede,
slow as the hammers on a ragtime piano.
The mill, full of crows' blinking eyes,
speed up, speedups, speed up—they squaw.

Cotton cannot grow any faster
but today the machines are competing with light.
Dust swarms in my sweat-soaked hair.
My body sags, warps like pooled glass.

UGLY JUG

Daddy's been in the ugly jug.
Them took it out in the woods.
Now Daddy thinks he is in love
with a squinty face toothy tight.

Them took it out in the woods.
They got a fire and all night
with a squinty face toothy tight.
The moon, tonight, shines so bright,

they got a fire and all night.
Them hammering on banjos
under a moon is shining bright.
Later the boys will come to blows.

Them hammering on banjos
falling over, laughing in stitches.
Later the boys will come to blows.
Mama's 'bout to pitch a fit.

Falling over, laughing in stitches,
now Daddy thinks he is in love.
Mama's 'bout to pitch a fit.
Daddy's been in the ugly jug.

CLIFF JUMP

Late August, we summer teens take Saturdays free.
We run over the rocky banks laughing in some
chase game; muscles flex, tense, stretch, climb
the steep—dig fingers into cracks, wrench ourselves up.

Mountain expanse of water calls up to us. My skin
tingles with nervousness as I look down the thirty feet.
"Take my hand," you tender, "We'll jump together."
Wind races round my feet! We send out seagull wails,

steal breath for the plunge. My body is a scream!
Down, down forever in bubbles, then buoyant, silent.
We are perch pulling ourselves up through the water.
We burst back into heat, howling out triumphant bellows.

SCREECH OWLS

We can only hear
their spotted throats:
shrill, warbling
their journey through pine
thicket in humming night.

We wonder if they know
their journey's end.
I wonder if we know ours.
This brood sings:
mountain, cornfield,
tomato patch. They think
nothing of tomorrow,
their ken consumed
with the hunt.

MUSCADINES
THE SOUTHERN GRAPE 1920

I. BROKEN ROOTS

Just past fourteen, managing eight sides
my knees thin beneath my dress, I piece
as the lion prowls the line with pride.

At final bell, I stray into his leer
as machines jerk, sputter—greedy beasts.
Then he's there, clutching, urging for a date
whispering of mill positions, he steers,
grips as the workers churn through the gates.

My heart lost, my mind fills with shrill bees,
I look around for escape
but it is too late, his hands on my knees.

II. RIPENING

Beneath the wheezing of the looms,
the spinning of the threads, my womb
begins hammering a dull beat,
a song of its own. I work sides
in trances, full of broken strings,
straining knots under the weight

of this hard little stone. The old
women pour tinctures of cotton
but their broken roots don't stop
its growth. I get Bill: "What you done?
I'm blowing up with your sin."
His knuckles sting across my cheek.
Straw boss thinks he'll beat it out
like I'm a rug thick with dirt.

III. STILL BIRTH

my curved stomach floats in hazy light
my gaze sweeps over the hall of machines
their thumping endless weaving
producing the stretched fabric of time

a young girl so blonde she's like bleached cotton
presses her ear to my belly with a low song
I catch her golden hair in my hands
and begin to spin—lives spool out like threads

I see other children, arms and legs darting
quartz faces spin, girls with salt in the corners
of their mouths, thin boys with dark crusty eyes
swaying like grasses in a fast-moving wind
are they calling my name?
Lindy Lee, Lindy Lee, Lindy Lee

* * *

My fingers sink in bloody slime. Machine dripping.
The straw boss kneels, holding a white stone.

IV. SNAPPED STRING

How much time passed—I don't know
as I swam in the mill hall heat
sweat-soaked, bloody, cotton-covered.
Till I heard Mama's voice boiling,
pulling the still stone from Bill's hands.

As many voices as leaves on a tree.
Hands, Mama's hands laying on that man
slapping his arms bloody till Pop
slides her into a pile of snapped string.

My brothers become an ocean
carrying me down the waves of stairs,
carrying me home to Mill Hill.

Yellow root, honey, and soakies.
Whiskey and cold-water baths.
Bed, bible, prayers to Jesus.
Rifles that wash away sin.

V. REVIVAL

I ain't been right. Dropping pickwheels,
jumping at a twitch. Mama's Methodist
church is full of whispers, turned cheeks.
Then I seen 'em setting up the big tent, assembling
an organ. They got a whole gospel choir
rehearsing "Jacob's Ladder." We gonna go,

Becky and all us girls, watch that clean Baptist preacher
bring us to Jesus. Lord knows, my heart needs it so.
Everyday I'm burning. I got the devil stinging in my eyes.
Dear Jesus, Lord! I need so badly to be healed!
Put me on a golden chain, put me on a golden chain.
Every link in Jesus' name. All my sins be taken away.

The preacher's eyes are blue as autumn clear skies;
Jesus is in him as he rides a chair clear over, tears
his shirt. He's jumping all around, clapping,
grasping people's hands *What you go' to do*
when the worlds on fire. Clap for me! Clap!
I'm raising up, singing, *Come a-long to the meeting*
in here tonight! The preacher's got both my hands
pulling me up on stage: "Testify! Can I get a witness!

Amen, sister! You're a sinner. You are washed
with forgiveness. Pray with me for this girl!"
I'm pushed to my knees, taken up by my shoulders
shaking, my feet dangle, tears stream down my cheeks.

"Pray for this sister!" And I am forgiven.
All the weavers, doffers, and smash hands, praying
for me with my limp body in the preacher's arms.

Come, thou font of every blessing,
tune thy heart to sing thy grace.
Streams of mercy never ceasing.
Louder, Jesus, praise.

CORNBREAD

Wheat withers in summer heat,
but dent corn is our life blood:
breakfast, lunch, and supper
stirred up by the littlest of the brood.
Toll milled, three bags in, three out.
Marched beneath hefty millstone
sweet, coarse, creamy, complex
like Rumpelstiltskin spinning hay
into gold, our silk haired, field ripened
beauty blossoms into winter sustenance.

MAMA'S MILL CHRISTMAS
1921

Their carols croon, crackle beneath mill hill eaves.
Shrill children laugh in new cap gun delight, darting
between flask-handed fathers, washing wire arches,
outhouses, gardens. Orange slices make smiles sweet.

Jarred apple butter, gold lemons, and glazed cherries.
Mimah, Ruby, Mabel, Ruth cooking black eyed peas,
glazing yams, peeling potatoes, whisking gravy.
Generations of secret family recipes.

In-laws, brothers, cousins, new wives, and grandchildren
bound by mistletoe, fancy paper, festive pine.
The worn floor boards shake, blessèd with so many kin.
Aunts giggle, pop homemade bottles of their sweet wine.

When the family is so stuffed, them can hardly roll,
Floyd gets his guitar. They all spill to the neighbors
to belt out the old songs with the village Noel.
While lanterns swing over festive civic labors,

the village joins voices in *Praise His Name;*
young hands couple in a long spinning chain.

SPRING SWIMMING
1922

Low turkey feet and ferns
whisper beneath leather.
Poplars purple as dusk,
he splashes creek water—
laughter. We turn the bend,
hopping the dogged rocks.

I hear the fall before
I see its steady sheet.
Still gritty from the mill,
we commit coarse cotton
to a mossy root knob.

Deep icy spring, another world:
silk, fish skin.
Pearly flowers of lint
eddy in drifts, blossom

from our whirling wet locks

as calloused hands journey

towards shadowy release.

SIGNS OF MARRIAGE

To find how many years till you become
a bride you must blow dandelion fluff,
count pinky creases, roast eggs, add up
bubbles from a submerged pitcher,
or catch an iridescent dragonfly.

To find his name, twist an apple stem,
wind yarn, draw beans from a bag,
dribble wax into water, or gaze at smoke
in a mason jar. Try reading cards, licking
buttercups, or find the first flower of spring
on a Wednesday. Knit him a sweater
with your hair in the wool to bind.

You will never marry if you leave a quilt
unfinished, or if someone sweeps over your feet.
To dream of his handsome face,
place wedding cake under your pillow.

INDEPENDENCE DAY

Bud, Wormy, and Rabbit pick mandolins.
Whistle and em's fiddling on the store porch.
Hop light ladies yo'cakes all dough
You needn't worry the dust won't blow!

I'm off whirling across hard clay
our hair slapping and blowing like hay.
The mill is quiet as a drought. Instead everybody
is shouting out, *Rack-a-ma rack-a-ma I say!*

Our faces are tomatoes in silky night air.
Jerome slips his thick hand in mine.
Becky hands us dripping icy lemonade
as we promenade through the crowd.

Stephenson shoots the sky green, gold, blue.
Oh Carolina girls tonight won't you sing a tune
and dance by the light of the crescent moon.
I'll dream of Jerome back in the weave room.

THE SUMMER OF TIGER
SWALLOW TAILS

"Look, three butterflies on that laurel.
We're all going to heaven," Mama says.
This wet summer splashes the green hill
in cone flowers and blushing azaleas.

A bright Tiger and blue mate swirl up
before her face. "Ooh Lindy's getting married,"
Becky delights as a giant alights on her fingers.
"Mama, I can't remember. Does that mean I live

to eighty or die young? Ooh, Mama. What's the sign?"
A cold winter comes or a good autumn crop.
Riches within reach or the fading of fondness.
Transient happiness lifts on a hundred lush wings.

Summer heat of color: orange, yellow, blue.
What new fortunes will this autumn blow?

GIFTS OF SILVER

I love to watch Jerome in the cool morning,
as he goes fishing. He stands upon the hill,
handsome in his work clothes—sailing
the transparent fly whipping through mist,
my man, so much heart in his eyes.

I remember when we first began.
When we kissed, he held my face.
He whittled me a little fan.
For our wedding, I even found some lace.
But the treasured pebble, my 16th birthday
he caught and cooked a silver trout
sprinkled lilies on my dress. That full day,
my lips savored his kiss of salt.

WEDDING CAKE

Becky can bake a pie, flakiest shell
but our cake confectioner is Aunt Joe
with metal tube and flower butter molds,
pouring jelly into red jiggling roses.

Women visit with sugar, molasses,
eggs, crystal ginger, and canned pineapple.
Ruby plays with Baby. I'm basting lace.
Aunt Joe beats gelatin into fondant.

Becky slips in the batter a gold foil ring
humming *When They Swing the Golden Bell.*
Old shoes, blue garters, holy blessed vows,
wedding revelations, honeymoon surprises.

Our mill house is bustling hips and shoulders:
recipes, secrets—home-grown superstitions.

PELICAN

What is it? The grand bird with giant wings.
Foreign flapping and smacking of curved jaws,
they had never seen such a mechanical animal.
Course they had never seen the beach or blue waves
that clatter against the hard horizon.

Then the beast plummeted to within inches
of the surface, glided over the sheet of river.
They stood beside the beating copper bell
like they had all the minutes in the world
their mouths gaping like clam shells in a low tide.
As if a thousand strings weren't calling their names,
as if mill machines weren't falling silent.
Boss man bellowed, "It's just a pelican!
So what! You fools!" But it was a plain wonder!
A fisherman's omen so far from the sea.

THE RUB

"Rhodes Mfg. Co., Lincolnton, N.C."

"This little girl like many others in this state is so small she has to stand on a box to reach her machine. She is regularly employed as a knitter in London [i.e., Loudon?] Hosiery Mills. Said she did not know how long she had worked there. Location: Loudon, Tennessee."

THE COTTON MILL'S SONG

Thread spinner. Loom weaver.
Cloth maker to the world.
Doffers. Smashers. Slashers.
Whipping, sweltering and worn.

It is true what they tell you. I am wicked
with my women weaving through throbbing
night under the electric lights. And, yes,
they say I am cruel for I have slaughtered

the little child and then brought another
to fill his place. And they tell you I am vile.
But my reply: in the cheeks of girls
and the ribs of toddlers I have instilled

the hollows of hunger. And still I will turn
to those indolent idealists who huff
at our speeding machines and say to them:

Come and show me a grander temple
to our industry with brick walls buzzing
through sunrises and hail storms and snap frost.
Show me another place where the indigent,

the illiterate, the slow, the widowed
are set to toil so assiduously in
sweat-soaked aprons and wild, dripping hair.
Spouting steam and thick oil, I cast long shadows

"A little spinner in a Georgia Cotton Mill. Location: Georgia."

across the mountains. I sing my swollen song
timbre as dulcimer strings. Flushed. Defiant.
Racing. Thumping. Heaving. On the floor cotton
coating my woman's skin, singing with hands
like wrens, fueling the machinery of America

and singing the way only a burdened
soul can sing with chin thrown forward
and heart sour as ukulele. Humming.
Beating a foot on the cotton covered pine.

Blood pumping to the pulse of the looms. Singing!
Singing the heavy, linty, violent
song of the worker. Sinewy, sweat-soaked,
proud to be thread spinner. Loom weaver.
Cloth Maker to the World.

THE TIMES NEWS. 50ᵀᴴ ANNIVERSARY EDITION.
Sunday December 30th, 1923.

Sampson, he rode into town in eighteen seventy-two
all lit up with mountain creek moonshine, dark corner
deep stilled, prepared for a battle royal with a Revenuer
who had dynamited his steel stovepipes and wood barrels.
"In the old days, moonshine was a frequent battle starter,"
Dr. Earle said, "with leggers' weekly arrival in town
from the upper county's remote mountains. Gunfights daily.
The rattle of whiskey glasses in main street saloons drowned
by the shattering of window panes by drunken brawlers."

Slash Go the Prices! Ukuleles. Banjo's. $2.00.
Cinema Tomorrow and Tuesday! What a New Wife Learned:
The drama of a wife who sought more than marriage could give!
Riding in a rented Ford, three teen boys of Brandon Mill,
enticed two girls with sweet wine after nine on Friday night.
 "Folk in the city nowadays are going about day
by day unmolested, busy with life and liberty,"
said Dr. Earle from his century old Georgian town house.

SLICE

He takes second base the way a train
burns a grade, all heft and pent speed,
jolting the baseman into the chalked clay.
The crowd in the painted pine grandstand
roars like a room of power looms
each time he skins the cowhide off,
launching rockets past outfielders
into muddy pastures.

Even at fifteen, a bruiser of a boy,
a strapping right-hander
from a deep bench of cotton mill boys,
who got their start with bare feet
scrambling across red clay diamonds
exploding rag balls with picker sticks.

He was crosscut and rough. A burly hurler,
a stout slugger who made more
rollin' cotton and playin' Textile ball
than he could in the minor league.
Lady Luck never churned him to the top.
But his shifts were light, his store credit vast:
a slice with an eternal bat and ball at his palm.

SISTER RUBY

Maybe it was the chocolates, books,
too long without work. Mama had let her go
to fourteen before the mill wants to know:
'where she's at?' Sister Ruby would hand sew

the most beautiful cotton dresses, darts
and pleats like from the big department store.
She'd sashay sweet, fresh as strawberry tart.
A doll with not a hint of cotton on her.

At the mill, she couldn't handle the crowd,
the machines, she marched right back out the steam.
This teen soft and airy as a marshmallow
could make kettle's boil over, skin like cream.

She was the mill town's own Aphrodite.
Perfume sweet as honeysuckle. Lips lush
as Garbo. She floated like a loose kite
in wind, delighted as though earth was heaven.

BROTHER'S MESS OF CROSSES

Converted at 16, when the dummy train
derailed to tip across his pregnant wife.
A holy roller, a Carolina spinner,
a brush arbor caller, an off-key gospel singer.

He took scarlet paint to moonshine jars, boulders,
pine trees, fences, and the neighbor's pig.
His front plot, he planted a mess of crosses
and built his own monolith with river rocks.

He didn't pay no mind to section leaders,
howled his only boss was the man in heaven.
He sent 10,000 message bottles down the Reedy
River, dreamed of taking Jesus to Mars and Jupiter.

BABY MICHAEL

My palm cupping your bobbing head,
you whimper, clutch my shabby sleeve.
Between the girls, I tuck you in bed
sighing as I go once more to weave.
As I'm running sets, I keep
your little fingers in my mind. Back
home at dusk, with the milk you need
I rock you once again to sleep.

WILD GREENS SOUP

Fingers of frost stretch across the windows.
Seasoned wood crackles in the wood stove
while I stir the last salty pork knuckle
with a handful of beans, wild greens
into a pot of well water just off the boil.
Fall's harvest now a collection of empty jars.

The cupboard's breath is dust and dead moths.
Each stir is more a wish as the day considers
getting warm, sweet herbs summon cravings.
Morning casts its pink sap over frost-risen clay
as I shepherd this thinly-feathered brood
towards the cotton-strewn spinning room.

Today we will piece broken strings,
weave cotton scraps to make them something whole.

HOP ALONG LITTLE CROW

I was scared of it—thought it was a haint
or diseased that adolescent crow marching
up the front porch railing—squawking.
I went to get the broom but Jerome held

up his rough hand for me to be still.
Once a man's felt hunger, seen his boy
shrivel on biscuit, knows the gnaw:
pain builds a dulcimer within the chest

that memory plays upon with a thimble.
Jerome spread out a crumble of cracker
and watched the orange mouth thump:
"Ah, Lindy, baby crow can't fly yet."

Struggle does not always make you harder.
Charity starts with a twang in the heart.

THE FOOD OF THE SOUL

Knowledge is the food
of the soul. So boss man
teach me. Teach me to make
collards unfurl their rosettes
after the hard freeze of November.
Teach me to stretch out this plot
to nourish nine children
the way you time punch my fingers
to card a little more machine each day.
Learn me how your own children
in their polished leather boots
fill their lunch pails to skip towards
the townie school
while mine own has lungs full of lint,
calloused soles black with machine oil
and three meals a day of dry cornbread.

Educate my red dirt heels on the ways
of the mill master, the juggle of figures,
your thin margins, your post-war tightening
of my belt buckle. Teach me the jargon to feed
your soul, remember me the gravy taste,
hand-round your control's salty flavor
and give me back our already lost children.

SONNETS AFTER THE MILL
MOTHER'S LAMENT 1927

"While we slave for the bosses, our children scream and cry."
—Ella Mae Wiggins, Union Activist (1900 – 1929)

"Young doffers in Mollahan Mills, Newberry, S.C. Dec. 3/08.
Location: Newberry, South Carolina"

PART I: LITTLE SISTER'S LAMENT

Of earth and vinegar, flowers, camphor
this house, we smell of it and it of us.
The wizened string beans low, pitiful fuss
with wantin' taters, field peas or mush. Pure
pressure seals us tight. Bless.
The kettle canned peppers smoldering heat
conspires with the fat back for fibs of meat.
A low spring of cornbread n' collard mess.

Dry honeycomb alight; more bees than hive.
Is this how man is baited into bear?
Desperate for respite beyond hard chairs
while our narrow mother hones her rag knife.
Hoping pressure will change with the weather
beyond close-knit, we're cooked down together.

PART II: JEROME'S LAMENT

A small plot of garden is all we got
each neighbor raises a different crop
one peas and beans, the other spuds and yams.
The women fillin' their Saturdays cannin'.
The harvest brings big corn shuckin' parties,
a draught of whiskey, perpetual duties.
Still eking our living from this red clay
after working twelve hours every day.

I'm bone tired but can't get on the level.
Rent. Store credit. I'm in debt to the devil.
My littl'ins lips split, skin red with lesions
pellagra disabling each dark season.
Hungry in work or hungry on the line
so comes a point, the union's worth tryin'.

PART III: LINDY LEE'S LAMENT

I need angels to sing a workers' psalm!
Payday's just lists of figures from the clerk.
Not two low cents I ever saw of work
and loonies gone to grease the boss's palm.

But Ella May, her pain, was like my own—
no shoes to fit our babies' growing feet,
just hungry mouth's pained-call for milk and meat,
each cry drowned by the machines' jilted moans.

Her ballads armed my heart; mill work ain't fair.
Each day my oldest babies forced to spin.
Let's stand together till us workers win.
I too long have known, the mill does not care.
So I'll stand the line against these straw men
for an honest day's pay, for the sides we tend.

BLUE PANES

Indigo, cobalt, azure. Protection
from the evil eye or wandering ghouls.
Cool icy streams. The color of heaven.
Jesus' robes. Hyacinth blooms.

I always loved those windows,
twenty years those blue eyes met mine,
a window to the soul. Mr. Stephenson sent
the boys up on ladders, smashing

laughing with each rain of blue tears.
Blue tick. Bluebird. Blueberry.
Shards settled in the grass and shone
in the streaming sun like a thousand eyes.

Who knew mortar could be spread
so fast? By day end we stood
in the fluorescent lights, surrounded
on all sides by endless brick.

But the debris called to us like jewels to crows.
We couldn't help but pick up the shards,
filling our aprons with textured glass
then stringing our porches with their blue song.

NO LINTHEADS

at our school. Not likely
to attend, to value education,
said the uptown folk.

Their shabbiness, gaping
spider webs of threads
at knees, elbows, chest.
Bad news. Barefooted. Dumb
as mountain mud.
Factory trash. Irish.
said the uptown folk.

The only book they've seen
is the bible. And they've not cracked
it. The noise of their hacking,
machine oil caked, filthy
with lice, with lint,
blistered, blue-lipped
said the uptown folk.

Skinny like scarecrows.
Whole village is an eyesore.
They can't learn. Their parents
are careless, selfish, illiterate.
Poor.

SPEAK WITH YOUR FEET

Cornbread boy—get on learning like a hawk
on a chicken. Bull frogs know the rain,
but you know your mama like a bug
arguing with a hen. Some say eagles are silent,

but your swagger won't let you be the Easter
rooster. Race out this red dirt mill town
like your shirt tails are afire. Your hungry
eyes speak the future. Why be dry as an empty
creek bottom, when you could be the pie taster
on the gravy train? The sea cannot be measured

with a soup spoon; cold hunger is hard to erase.
Cornbread boy! Wag your own tail. Beat
your linty, dusty life! Sweep clean.
Don't let that straw boss put a spider

in your biscuit. Hobo yourself to the city.
Blood is thick, but Cornbread boy—get out.
A sigh goes farther than a shout.

THE BEST YEAR IN THE MOVIES

"All the good that ever came into this world
came from fools with faith."
Mr. Smith Goes to Washington

Lips red as Garbo. Struggling for a cause.
Dancing, dancing, and falling against love
in Paris, New York, traveling the globe
with Fred Astaire, all the time with perfect hair.

Dorothy, I too want to go home.
I want to prance lint-less.
I want to click my heels, glittered and gay
not dripping sweat at the frame.

1939. This mean, pitiful decade
will soon exhale, while America stretches
towards another war, the wretched
depression still at our door.

I'm sixteen. I click my heels
6 days a week. I've never felt
silk stockings or perfumed hand crème.
D.C. capital seems like a dream.

Its 1939—the Best Year in Movies.
I'll be the movie heroine and you,
you be Fred Astaire, we'll go dancing
dancing, dancing, all the time with perfect hair.

LABOR SHORTAGE

Big man says we got a labor shortage.
Lord, I know they've been forcing production
giving us yellow milky eyes, chapped fingers.

So then here's the yard men
carding inside. I felt my mouth open
n' close like a hooked brim,
swaying among the reams of white
in fluorescent lights.

But they keep to themselves
and us to our own.
Well, we wave n' hello
cause most we know,
and production's so short.

Monty been here long as any: loading the dummy
in a rusting forklift. They're killing our boys
in this war faster than God can make them.

I'm not growing extra arms
so let them folk get a place
inhaling cotton dust.

MIDDLE SALUDA

Lindy would not get out of the car.
The water licked her mirrors,
salivated over backseat groceries.
Cars gathered on the high side

of the road. He stamped his boots
into the swelling river road;
the gritty waters eddied round knees,
thighs then stomach. Rain rifted

off his hat, dove down his shirt.
Ma'am, your car is done. Let it go.
Glass shattered, disappeared in rain.
Nature salts our treasures.

Hand stiff as a hook, it shook
at the back of his neck. A plastic
grocery bag bettied her head,
her flowered dress waterlogged.

She moaned as the car banged
over the bridge, grocery bags
balanced like swans. Turning away
a herd of cows crowded on a grass plot.

LAST DAY AT THE MILL

I have whirled my life out in whistle bells
but tomorrow I will take up silk.

I will pull bills from my mason jar
squirreled home behind the washer.

Forty years a spot of gold
fell by my machine. I held

my aching fingers in its warmth.
Where has that tiny globe gone?

My pink shirt—cool, coarse cotton
these hands have touched ten thousand, more.

I've stitched finishes into biscuits and birthdays
but tomorrow I will lay it down.

Tomorrow I will take up silk.

WE WALK ON THE MOON

The air hung electric on our stooped shoulders.
Jerome picked mandolin over foreign TV voices.
We all counted down, held our breath, sighed it out,
a collective heave. Neil Armstrong walking

with our fingerprints on his Teflon-coated-thread suit.
Standing shoulder to shoulder on the porch, mesmerized
by the RCA Heralder, we melded together into Teflon
with dusty regolith below our feet, our heads light

with triumph. The cold moon air brushed against us
sending stars across our arms. Cotton cart wheeled over
swimming oceans. A million pin pricks in dark fabric
swallowed us and our lifetime of long textile shifts

transforming our work worn hands into things that mattered
as we stood on the moon in the earth's shifting brightness.

GRANDMA LEE

Grandma Lee says life blurs like trees past a window, mirrors
become thieves, years roll like miles on a spinning odometer.

We want to be high-up, she told the man at the little place.
We want the sunrise to warm across our bodies.

On the top floor of the mausoleum, their names curl
in silver, white plots rise like condominiums.

Grandma Lee wonders who will give the service.
The Methodist preacher is about dead already.

She presses her heel onto the shovel, turning black dirt
to plant peppers and tomatoes. She pulls up a garlic stalk,

presses the fragrant bulb to her nose. She pickles hot peppers
and jars Carolina peaches for the shortest days of the year.

LINDY LEE'S SKY QUEENS

"Old Turkey Buzzard come flopping down the hollow.
Lend me your wings to fly across the river to my Lord."
—Appalachian Ballad

I been sitting here an hour watching them stretch
their white fingers. Up there they swing, dark sky queens
riding invisible up currents of rich sky and lemon sun.

Rubber faces and prickly eyes masked by height,
these undomesticated birds breast the blue
then stoop to earth for mortality's small scraps.

I sit here scarred, twisted—waiting to feel my hard
fingers stretch through burning blue, twirling and glory bound.

THE COLD

The sheets are left on the bed as the family packs
first aid kits, the worn leather Bible, Octagon soap
and underclothes. Lindy wonders if they should
unplug the appliances or cover the sofa with plastic.

The sirens drone and the children cry. Ripe
tomatoes and bushy azaleas glow crimson and pink.
As their Plymouth pulls out the drive, they think
of the protection guide, the Tang and the waterless

hand cleaner. They have heard about the ration
crackers, canned meat, and carbohydrate supplements.
But they do not allocate thoughts for loss:
jays and robins dropping in the poisoned air,

the quiet claustrophobia of the fallout shelter,
the eerie haloes of flashlights on 1600 faces,
the blooming stench, the smell of panic.

HISTORY AND PROCESS

These poems began with a photograph. I was hosting a workshop on poetry inspired by family history using old photographs as prompts. One of my sample photographs was of a woman working at a textile machine. Memories of family stories flooded my mind, and I wrote a poem: "Last Day at the Mill." A personal obsession with the Southern textile industry, and more importantly the culture it engendered, was born.

Yet as I considered this history, I realized that I had always had a connection to it. This industry brought my father, a machine tool engineer, from England via Boston to Greenville, SC—the textile capital of the world. I grew to thrive in its landscape of smoke stacks, water towers, and red-brick mills with acres of pine floors. Grandmothers and uncles shared mill stories at family gatherings. In third grade, I won first place in the Stone Manufacturing poster contest with my original slogan, "People sleep cozily with American textiles." I even had my picture taken with the mayor at the award ceremony.

As my passion for the mills and their people grew, I began talking to family and community members who had worked at Union Bleachery, Brandon Mill, Poe Mill and Slater Mill in the Upcountry of South Carolina. They painted a picture of tight-knit communities, the mill villages of women who had always been in the workplace, of a paradoxical life, both industrial and rural.

In 2005, a photographer invited me to visit Courtney Mill in Newry, SC. The original shift bell with its inscription struck me on a visceral level: "I arouse the slothful, I call the people to work. I announce the Sabbath Day, I warn ye how your time passes away. Serve God, therefore, while life doth last, And say, 'Gloria in Excelsis Deo.'"

Before that moment, I had no idea how much power the Mill owners had over the lives of their workers. My second mill poem, SHIFT BELL: A FOUND POEM, was born.

During the summer of 2005, I began my research in earnest. I read *Textile Town* (Spartanburg: Hub City, 2002). I scoured the Greenville County Library and Clemson University Libraries pouring over microfiche archives of local newspapers from the 1920s and 1930s and discovering history books such as Victoria Beyerly's *Hard Times Cotton Mill Girls* (NY: Cornell, 1986) and *Like a Family* (Chapel Hill: UNCP, 1987)

I unearthed priceless and rare recordings of interviews with textile workers from across the Southern Piedmont. And, most rewarding of all, I talked to the retired textile workers who still lived in my community.

As I began to synthesize information from these diverse sources, I noticed patterns of shared history. Struggles, structures, and institutions of mill life were much the same in towns across the piedmont region of the South.

This important history had been one largely unfamiliar to me despite growing up in a mill town. These community mill folk were left out of the "canonized" historical timeline. Their stories reduced to a footnote of Southern history, a scholarly afterthought. I realized that my picture of life in America after the turn of the 19th century was based on curricular books, which mostly depicted the north in novels like *The Great Gatsby, The Jungle,* and *A Tree Grows in Brooklyn.*

As I continued to delve into this comparatively neglected history, I found my preconceived notions being shattered. The first was that white women did not work outside the home until the years of the Second World War and more generally the 1960's. Yet, here were whole factories of white women and children working from the 1890's forward. The second draw-dropping fact was that while these workers had an hourly rate, these Americans were not actually being paid. They were de facto indentured servants—for after their rent, utilities, and food staples were deducted from their pay checks, they were generally in-debt as they started their next pay period. In debt, even though they were still growing most of their own food and working twelve hour shifts in the mill. And the few families who had enough workers in the household to draw some pay (mostly supervisors) were given only tokens or scripts.

My third perception that was challenged was that the United States had always been a democracy, or at least a democratic republic informed by the ideals of the Founding Fathers. Yet, here were rural mill villages governed in practice by despots in the form of mill owners, to the degree they even printed their own money redeemable only at mill stores where they determined the prices and inventory. Mill owners were unelected legislators, education superintendents, church bishops, and retail monopolies all rolled into one. In fact, during the height of the textile mill era, the governors of North Carolina, South Carolina, and Georgia were all mill owners. And yes, textile mills received tax breaks from the states for setting up their own schools (ending at sixth grade), but this insular and unaccredited education barred mill worker's children from enrolling at state high schools. Control made cotton king.

Despite my initial outrage, I came to share the equivocal view of the mill workers towards the patriarchal textile industry. A view that balanced industrial progress with workers' rights. A view that celebrated these communities that overcame adversity together. A view that embraced the relative comfort and rights that came after 1945. To date, the textile industry shaped and continues to define the Southern landscape more strongly than any other industry. The symbols of their survival are the water towers and smoke stacks still punctuating our horizons.

I hope that my poems serve as a beacon that shines a light on the unrecognized women, children, and men who selflessly fueled the growth of industry throughout the South. This is their story.

Kimberly F. Simms

ABOUT KIMBERLY

Kimberly's literary voice is rooted in the Southern tradition of storytelling, informed by her British and Southern lineage. She is an award-winning poet who entertains and educates with poetry that is both poignant and inspiring.

She was the 2016 Carl Sandburg National Historic Site Writer-In-Residence (Flat Rock, NC); she is a member of the SC Humanities Council's Speaker's Bureau and a pioneer in the world of poetry slam.

A graduate of Furman University (BA) and Clemson University (MA), her work has appeared in over 30 literary journals including the *Asheville Poetry Review* and the *Broad River Review*. She is a Pushcart Prize nominee and her work is included in the South Carolina Poetry Archives at Furman University.

She is the proud founder of Wits End Poetry, a non-profit now celebrating 15 years of creating South Carolina poetry events and educational outreach. When not writing, you'll find Kimberly hiking and raising her chickens. For more about Kimberly and her work:

www.kimberlyjsimms.com

ABOUT LEWIS HINE

Lewis was born in Oshkosh, Wisconsin on September 26, 1874. Initially, he started his career as a school teacher in New York City but discovered his true calling was that of photographer. In 1908, Hine became the official photographer for the National Child Labor Committee as they worked to outlaw child exploitation. Travelling with an old-fashioned box camera, Hine often used deception to gain entry to plants to photograph child workers. He told factory owners that he was a fire inspector, bible salesman, or machine photographer to gain entry. If his ruse failed, Hine would wait outside the factory gates to photograph children as they came and went.

Unfortunately, in the 1930's Hine fell on hard times. By 1938, Hine had lost his home and was living on public assistance as he was unable to gain photography assignments. He died in 1940 in poverty at the age of 66, just one year after his wife passed away. Today his photography is revered but not widely known despite the haunting history it captures.

Information gleaned from the National Child Committee Collection's "Background Information" provided by the Library of Congress on their website www.loc.gov.

DISCUSSION QUESTIONS

1. How did the landscape effect the lives of the mill workers in the Southern Piedmont?

2. Why do you think parents allowed their children to work in the textile mills?

3. How did you experience the main character, Lindy Lee? How did her experiences make you feel?

4. In the poem cycle "Muscadines," why do you think Lindy Lee kept quiet about what Bill (her boss) did to her?

5. The conditions in the textile mills were tough. If you were a textile worker during this time, would you rather move from village to village looking for better opportunity OR stay in one village your whole life?

6. Do you think the history of the mill villages still influences southern culture today? If so, how?

7. Why was religion so important to some textile mill workers?

8. What was your favorite poem in the collection? How did you connect to it?

www.ingramcontent.com/pod-product-compliance
Lightning Source LLC
Chambersburg PA
CBHW021200090426
42740CB00008B/1175